WORKBOOK

for

Unlock The Hidden Leader

A practice guide on Become the Leader You Were Destined to Be

Aviana Print

Table of content

How to Use This Workbook

Welcome to the companion workbook for [Title of the Original Book]. This workbook has been designed to help you dive deeper into the content of the original book, gain a better understanding of its key concepts, and apply them to your life. Whether you've already read the book or you're just starting, this workbook is a valuable resource to enhance your learning experience.

Workbook Overview

Summary of the Original Book: Begin your journey by revisiting the core ideas and messages of the original book. This section provides a concise summary, allowing you to refresh your memory and establish a solid foundation for the exercises and reflections that follow.

Chapter Key Lessons: As you progress through the workbook, you'll find sections dedicated to each chapter of the original book. In these sections, we've distilled the key lessons and insights from each chapter. Pay close attention to these summaries, as they serve as a roadmap for your self-improvement journey.

Self-Reflection Questions: After reviewing the chapter's key lessons, take the time to reflect on your own experiences and thoughts. We've provided thought-provoking self-reflection questions that encourage you to apply the book's concepts to your life. Use these questions to explore your personal insights, beliefs, and actions.

Self-Evaluation Questions: Towards the end of this workbook, you'll encounter a dedicated section for self-evaluation. Here, you can assess your progress and growth in light of the book's teachings. These questions are designed to help you measure your development and identify areas where further exploration or improvement may be necessary.

Checklist: To keep yourself organized and accountable, we've included a checklist. Use it to track your completion of each chapter's exercises and self-reflection questions. This checklist will help you stay on course and ensure you don't miss any critical steps in your self-improvement journey.

Getting the Most Out of This Workbook

To maximize the benefits of this workbook, consider the following tips:

Read the Original Book: If you haven't already, we recommend reading or revisiting the original book before using this workbook. This will provide you with a comprehensive understanding of the author's ideas.

Set Aside Dedicated Time: Allocate regular, uninterrupted time to work through this workbook. Reflecting on your thoughts and experiences can be a deeply rewarding process, but it requires focus and commitment.

Be Honest with Yourself: When answering self-reflection questions and completing self-evaluations, be honest and open with yourself. Growth often begins with self-awareness.

Connect with Others: Consider discussing your insights and reflections with friends, a book club, or an online community. Sharing your thoughts can lead to richer discussions and new perspectives.

Remember that this workbook is a tool for personal growth and exploration. It's here to guide you, challenge you, and ultimately help you apply the valuable lessons from the original book to your life. We encourage you to engage with it thoughtfully and consistently, and we wish you a transformative journey ahead.

INTRODUCTION

Leadership is more than a desk or a title on a business card. It isn't about barking instructions from the top or having the loudest voice in the room.

At its foundation, leadership is about inspiration, motivation, and the capacity to bring out the best in oneself and others. It is about acknowledging that everyone of us have leadership potential that needs to be awakened, fostered, and unleashed.

In his fascinating book "Unlock The Hidden Leader: Become The Leader You Were Destined To Be," Gifford Thomas questions traditional views of leadership. He asks us to engage on a revolutionary journey in which we reimagine leadership as a force that transcends typical age, gender, and background barriers.

Thomas shows the way to being a leader who inspires and empowers, regardless of official titles or positions, via his thought-provoking thoughts and real-world experiences.

You are taking a huge step toward uncovering your latent leadership potential as you hold this unofficial companion workbook in your hands. This workbook is more than simply a supplement to the book; it is a roadmap, a guide, and a companion on your journey to become the leader you were born to be. Whether you're reading Thomas' book for the first time or revisiting it with new eyes, this workbook will help you go deeper, ponder more deeply, and act more meaningfully on the concepts stated in the book.

What is the purpose of a workbook?

"Why do I need a workbook to go with a leadership book?" you may be thinking. The answer is found in the transforming power of active participation. Reading a book is a rewarding experience, but the true magic arrives when you internalize and apply its lessons to your life. The workbook acts as a link between knowledge and action, transforming smart ideas into measurable outcomes.

This unofficial workbook is intended to serve as a friend, mentor, and accountability partner for you. It includes organized activities, self-reflection questions, and practical tools to help you navigate the book's chapters and successfully investigate, comprehend, and apply the ideas of hidden leadership. This workbook adjusts to your requirements whether you are reading the book alone, in a group, or even leading a conversation.

Summary

Chapter 1: The Hidden Leader

In this chapter, Thomas challenges the traditional definition of leadership. He argues that leadership is not about authority, position, or title. It is about the ability to inspire and motivate others to achieve great things. He says that everyone has the potential to be a leader, regardless of their age, gender, or background.

Chapter 2: The Qualities of a Great Leader

In this chapter, Thomas discusses the qualities of a great leader. He says that great leaders are:

Visionary: They have a clear vision for the future and the ability to communicate that vision to others.

Inspiring: They have the ability to motivate and excite others to follow them.

Courageous: They are not afraid to take risks and stand up for what they believe in.

Decisive: They are able to make quick and decisive decisions.

Communicative: They are able to communicate effectively with others.

Trustworthy: They are honest and reliable.

Servant-Leaders: They put the needs of others before their own.

Chapter 3: Discovering Your Leadership Potential

In this chapter, Thomas helps you to discover your leadership potential. He asks you a series of questions to help you identify your strengths, weaknesses, and interests. He also helps you to define your personal leadership brand.

Chapter 4: Developing Your Leadership Skills

In this chapter, Thomas provides you with a step-by-step guide on how to develop your leadership skills. He covers a variety of topics, including communication, delegation, decision-making, and conflict resolution.

Chapter 5: Building Your Leadership Network

In this chapter, Thomas explains the importance of building a strong leadership network. He shows you how to connect with other leaders, learn from them, and get their support.

Chapter 6: Taking Action and Leading Others

In this chapter, Thomas encourages you to take action and start leading others. He provides you with tips on how to motivate and inspire others, and how to overcome challenges.

Chapter 7: The Power of One

In this chapter, Thomas reminds you that even one person can make a difference. He shares stories of ordinary people who have made extraordinary things happen.

Chapter 8: The Future of Leadership

In this chapter, Thomas discusses the future of leadership. He argues that the traditional top-down leadership model is no longer effective. He says that we need to move towards a more collaborative and inclusive style of leadership.

Overall, Unlock The Hidden Leader is a practical and inspiring guide to becoming a great leader. It is a must-read for anyone who wants to make a difference in the world.

Here are some additional thoughts on the book:

I appreciate Thomas's emphasis on the importance of servant leadership. I believe that this is the most effective way to lead others.

I also like the way Thomas challenges the traditional definition of leadership. He makes a convincing case that anyone can be a leader, regardless of their age, gender, or background.

I think the book is well-written and easy to follow. The stories and anecdotes that Thomas shares are also helpful and inspiring.

The Hidden Leader

key lessons

1. Leadership Goes Beyond Authority: Traditional definitions of leadership frequently associate it with positions of power, titles, or seniority. Chapter 1 stresses, however, that leadership is not limited to such responsibilities. It emphasizes that leadership is ultimately about the ability to inspire and encourage others and that this can be performed by anyone of any age, gender, or background.

2. Leadership Is Inherent in Everyone: The chapter emphasizes the concept that everyone possesses leadership potential. It calls into question the concept that leadership is a unique quality held by a chosen few. Instead, it implies that everyone has the potential to become a leader and make a big difference in their own way.

3. Inspiration and Motivation Are Critical: Effective leaders inspire and motivate people to achieve greatness. It is not about issuing orders, but about persuading people to behave gladly. This lecture stresses the significance of communication and inspiration as key components of leadership.

4. Leadership Diversity: Chapter 1 urges readers to appreciate that leadership is not limited to a certain group or background. It recognizes the diversity of possible leaders and believes that a more inclusive approach to leadership can result in more rich and imaginative solutions.

5. Leadership as a Personal Journey: The chapter introduces the concept of leadership as a personal journey of development and progress. It emphasizes that being a leader is not a one-size-fits-all process, but rather a discovery of one's unique qualities, values, and potential. This lesson encourages readers to embrace their uniqueness as they embark on their leadership path.

Self-Reflection Question

1. What is your current definition of leadership, and how has it changed since you read Chapter 1?

_____

_____

_____

_____

_____

_____

_____

_____

_____

_____

_____

_____

_____

_____

_____

_____

_____

_____

2. Can you think of a moment when someone, regardless of title or position, motivated you to act or make beneficial changes? What characteristics did they have that made them leaders at the time?

_____

_____

_____

_____

_____

_____

_____

_____

_____

_____

_____

_____

_____

_____

_____

_____

_____

_____

_____

3. Consider your own life. Have you ever operated as a leader, even if it was in a tiny way, without a formal leadership position?

_____

_____

_____

_____

_____

_____

_____

_____

_____

_____

_____

_____

_____

_____

_____

_____

_____

_____

_____

_____

_____

4. Do you feel that leadership is a natural ability that certain individuals are born with, or do you believe that everyone can be a leader? What is your reasoning?

_____

_____

_____

_____

_____

_____

_____

_____

_____

_____

_____

_____

_____

_____

_____

_____

5. Think about a leader you admire. What aspects of that leader's personality or deeds inspire you, and how can you adopt some of those characteristics into your leadership style, regardless of your present position?

_____

_____

_____

_____

_____

_____

_____

_____

_____

_____

_____

_____

_____

_____

_____

_____

6. Have you ever felt confined or held back in your personal or professional life because you did not feel you were a typical leader? How may Chapter 1's leadership viewpoint influence your attitude toward similar situations?

_____

_____

_____

_____

_____

_____

_____

_____

_____

_____

_____

_____

_____

_____

_____

_____

7. Consider the variety of people in your life. What influence may the concept that leadership transcends age, gender, and background have on your interactions and partnerships with others?

_____

_____

_____

_____

_____

_____

_____

_____

_____

_____

_____

_____

_____

_____

_____

_____

The Qualities of A Great Leader

Key lessons

1. Visionary Leadership: Great leaders have a clear vision for the future and the ability to successfully share that vision to inspire others.

2. Inspiration and Motivation: They are excellent at motivating and thrilling others, causing them to follow them gladly rather than obediently.

3. Bold Decision-Making: Great leaders are not afraid to take calculated risks and stand firm in the face of uncertainty or resistance.

4. Decisiveness: They can make rapid and confident judgments, which builds trust and accelerates development.

5. Effective Communication and Trustworthiness: Effective leaders are effective communicators who foster trust by being honest, dependable, and transparent.

Self- Reflection Question

1.Think about a leader you admire. What is their future vision, and how do they express it to inspire others?

_____

_____

_____

_____

_____

_____

_____

_____

_____

_____

_____

_____

_____

_____

_____

_____

_____

2. Consider a period when a leader influenced you. What acts or words compelled you to act? How might comparable motivational approaches be incorporated into your leadership style?

_____

_____

_____

_____

_____

_____

_____

_____

_____

_____

_____

_____

_____

_____

_____

_____

_____

_____

_____

3. Have you ever been hesitant to decide because you were afraid or uncertain? What can you learn from the notion of brave decision-making, and how can you overcome such reservations in the future?

_____

_____

_____

_____

_____

_____

_____

_____

_____

_____

_____

_____

_____

_____

_____

_____

_____

4. Consider your decision-making process. Do you have any places where you pause or second-guess yourself? How can you become more decisive in such circumstances?

_____

_____

_____

_____

_____

_____

_____

_____

_____

_____

_____

_____

_____

_____

_____

_____

_____

_____

_____

5. Consider the leaders you admire. What communication tactics do they employ to establish trust and credibility? How can you

improve your communication skills as a leader to become more trustworthy?

_____

_____

_____

_____

_____

_____

_____

_____

_____

_____

_____

_____

_____

_____

_____

_____

_____

_____

6. Evaluate your leadership abilities. Which of the attributes described in Chapter 2 do you believe you already have, and which do you believe you should improve on?

_____

_____

_____

_____

_____

_____

_____

_____

_____

_____

_____

_____

_____

_____

_____

_____

_____

_____

_____

7. Identify a role model that represents some of the excellent leadership attributes discussed in Chapter 2. What specific acts or behaviors of this role model can you mimic to strengthen your leadership abilities?

Discovering Your Leadership Potential

Key Lessons:

1. Self-Discovery: The importance of self-discovery in leadership is emphasized in Chapter 3. Knowing your talents, limitations, and interests is essential for good leadership.

2. Personal Leadership Brand: You'll discover the importance of developing your personal leadership brand, which distinguishes you as a distinct leader with a different character and style.

3. Self-Assessment and Reflection: The chapter emphasizes regular self-assessment and reflection to improve your leadership potential.

4. Leveraging Strengths: Embrace and exploit your strengths to become a more effective leader.

5. Constant growth and refining: Leadership potential is not static; it requires constant growth and refining.

6. Values Definition: Identify your key values and how they match with your leadership style.

7. Self-Confidence: Self-confidence is an important component of reaching your leadership potential.

Self-Reflection Questions

1. How well do I now understand my leadership skills, shortcomings, and interests?

_____

_____

_____

_____

_____

_____

_____

_____

_____

_____

_____

_____

_____

_____

_____

_____

_____

2. What areas of my personal and professional life represent my distinctive leadership brand, and how can I strengthen it?

_____

_____

_____

_____

_____

_____

_____

_____

_____

_____

_____

_____

_____

_____

_____

_____

_____

_____

3. What approaches or tools can I use to conduct regular self-evaluation and reflection on my leadership journey?

_____

_____

_____

_____

_____

_____

_____

_____

_____

_____

_____

_____

_____

_____

_____

_____

_____

4. Explain how you can actively use your skills to become a better leader?

_____

_____

_____

_____

_____

_____

_____

_____

_____

_____

_____

_____

_____

_____

_____

_____

_____

5. What efforts can you make to guarantee that your leadership qualities continue to grow and develop?

_____

_____

_____

_____

_____

_____

_____

_____

_____

_____

_____

_____

_____

_____

_____

_____

6. Have your basic values been discovered and expressed, and how do they affect your leadership style?

_____

_____

_____

_____

_____

_____

_____

_____

_____

_____

_____

_____

_____

_____

_____

_____

7. What tactics can you use to boost and sustain your self-esteem in your leadership roles?

_____

_____

_____

_____

_____

_____

_____

_____

_____

_____

_____

Developing Your Leadership Skills

Key Lessons:

1. Skill Development: In Chapter 4, the significance of polishing particular leadership abilities such as communication, delegation, decision-making, and conflict resolution is emphasized.

2. Continuous Learning: Leadership is a lifelong process of learning and progress.

3. Practical Advice: This chapter offers practical advice and tactics for improving critical leadership abilities.

4. Adaptability: Effective leaders are capable of adapting their talents to a variety of contexts and obstacles.

5. Effective Communication: Effective communication is essential for leadership success.

6. Delegation and Empowerment: Learning to delegate responsibilities and empower people is essential for developing as a leader.

7. Conflict Resolution: Team leaders must be skilled at managing and resolving disagreements.

Self-Reflection Questions

1. Which of the specific leadership abilities outlined in Chapter 4 do you feel are your strengths, and which do you believe need improvement?

_____

_____

_____

_____

_____

_____

_____

_____

_____

_____

_____

_____

_____

_____

_____

_____

_____

2. In your leadership career, how do you now emphasize ongoing learning and skill improvement?

_____

_____

_____

_____

_____

_____

_____

_____

_____

_____

_____

_____

_____

_____

_____

_____

3. What practical efforts can you take to improve your communication skills and increase their effectiveness in a leadership setting?

_____

_____

_____

_____

_____

_____

_____

_____

_____

_____

_____

_____

_____

_____

_____

_____

_____

4. Do you have a systematic approach to decision-making when presented with difficult choices, and how can you enhance it?

_____

_____

_____

_____

_____

_____

_____

_____

_____

_____

_____

_____

_____

_____

_____

_____

_____

_____

5. Are there specific resources, courses, or mentors that can help you develop your leadership skills further?

_____

_____

_____

_____

_____

_____

_____

_____

_____

_____

_____

_____

_____

_____

_____

_____

_____

6. How comfortable are you with delegation, and what strategies can you implement to empower team members more effectively?

_____

_____

_____

_____

_____

_____

_____

_____

_____

_____

_____

_____

_____

_____

_____

_____

_____

_____

7. Reflect on past instances of conflict within your teams or groups. What can you learn from those experiences to improve your conflict resolution skills?

_____

_____

_____

_____

_____

_____

_____

_____

Building Your Leadership Network

Key Lessons:

1. The need for Networking: Chapter 5 emphasizes the need to develop a strong leadership network.

2. Learning from Others: Networking allows you to learn from the experiences and perspectives of other leaders.

3. Support System: A strong network may be a significant resource for you as you embark on your leadership path.

4. Mentorship: Seek guidance from experienced executives who can mentor you.

5. Mutual Benefits: Networking is a two-way street; you give and get help.

6. Online and Offline Networking: Look into both online and offline networking opportunities to develop your leadership network.

7. Nurturing connections: An effective leadership network is built on connections.

Self-Reflection Questions

1. How would you define the present condition of your leadership network, and where may it be strengthened?

_____

_____

_____

_____

_____

_____

_____

_____

_____

_____

_____

_____

_____

_____

_____

_____

_____

2. Can you identify people in your network who could act as mentors or advisers to you on your path to leadership?

_____

_____

_____

_____

_____

_____

_____

_____

_____

_____

_____

_____

_____

_____

_____

_____

_____

3. How actively do you seek chances to learn from and share your views with other leaders?

_____

_____

_____

_____

_____

_____

_____

_____

_____

_____

_____

_____

_____

_____

_____

_____

_____

_____

4. Think of times when your network has helped or guided you in your leadership responsibilities.

_____

_____

_____

_____

_____

_____

_____

_____

_____

_____

_____

_____

_____

_____

_____

_____

_____

5. Are there any leaders or experts you admire and want to engage with? How can you make contact or start a collaboration?

_____

_____

_____

_____

_____

_____

6. How do you balance your online and offline networking activities, and how can you maximize both for your objectives?

_____

_____

_____

_____

_____

_____

_____

_____

7. What techniques can you use to cultivate and sustain excellent connections within your leadership network?

_____

_____

_____

_____

_____

_____

_____

_____

_____

_____

_____

Taking Action and Leading Others

Key Lessons:

1. Leadership necessitates action: Chapter 6 highlights the importance of taking action and motivating others to do the same.

2. Setting High expectations: Effective leaders establish high expectations for themselves and lead by example.

3. Motivation and Inspiration: This chapter discusses how to motivate and inspire people to attain common goals.

4. Overcoming Obstacles: Leaders must be resilient in the face of adversity.

5. Decision-Making: Making educated and timely decisions is critical for effective leadership.

6. Empowering Team Members: Empowering team members promotes a sense of ownership and accountability.

7. Feedback and Recognition: Giving constructive feedback and acknowledging accomplishments are crucial leadership behaviors.

Self-Reflection Questions

1. Consider your recent leadership responsibilities. What actions and examples have you used to illustrate your leadership?

_____

_____

_____

_____

_____

_____

_____

_____

_____

_____

_____

_____

_____

_____

_____

_____

_____

2. In your personal and professional lives, how do you now encourage and inspire people, and how might you improve these skills?

_____

_____

_____

_____

_____

_____

_____

_____

_____

_____

_____

_____

_____

_____

_____

_____

_____

3. Think of a major struggle or setback you've experienced as a leader. How did you get through it, and what did you gain from it?

4. In your leadership responsibilities, how do you approach decision-making, and how can you strengthen this part of your leadership style?

_____

_____

_____

_____

_____

_____

_____

_____

_____

_____

_____

_____

_____

_____

_____

_____

5. Consider the dynamics of your team. How can you encourage team members to assume greater responsibility and ownership?

_____

_____

_____

_____

_____

_____

_____

_____

_____

_____

_____

_____

_____

_____

_____

_____

_____

6. Examine your feedback and recognition procedures. Do you properly deliver constructive comments and appreciate accomplishments?

_____

_____

_____

_____

_____

_____

_____

_____

_____

_____

_____

_____

_____

_____

_____

_____

7. Can you think of a leader whose activities have inspired you? What characteristics or acts made them inspirational?

_____

_____

_____

_____

_____

_____

_____

_____

_____

The Power of One

Key Lessons:

1. Individual influence: In Chapter 7, it is stressed that even one individual may have a large beneficial influence.

2. Inspiring Stories: This chapter tells the stories of ordinary people who accomplished great things through their deeds.

3. Small Acts of Compassion and Initiative Matter: Small acts of compassion and initiative may have a beneficial ripple effect.

4. Empowerment: Acknowledge your ability to create change and motivate others to do the same.

5. Passion and dedication: The power of one is frequently the result of intense passion and unflinching dedication.

6. Overcoming Doubts: With perseverance and faith in your purpose, you may overcome doubts and challenges.

7. Collective Impact: The aggregate influence of individual activities can result in significant collective change.

Self-Reflection Questions

1. Can you recall any instances in your own life in which a single action or choice had a large influence on you or others?

_____

_____

_____

_____

_____

_____

_____

_____

_____

_____

_____

_____

_____

_____

_____

_____

_____

_____

2. Consider the chapter's stories of ordinary people doing amazing feats. What impact have these stories had on your perception of the power of one?

_____

_____

_____

_____

_____

_____

_____

_____

_____

_____

_____

_____

_____

_____

_____

_____

3. What simple activities or efforts can you do in your community or company to bring about good change?

_____

_____

_____

_____

_____

_____

_____

_____

_____

_____

_____

_____

_____

_____

_____

_____

_____

4. Think of a cause or interest that you care greatly about. How can you use your passion to promote change and set a good example?

_____

_____

_____

_____

_____

_____

_____

_____

_____

_____

_____

_____

_____

_____

_____

_____

5. Have you ever had doubts or met barriers in your efforts to make a difference? How did you get past them?

_____

_____

_____

_____

_____

_____

_____

_____

_____

_____

_____

_____

_____

_____

_____

_____

_____

_____

6. Consider the notion of collaborative influence. How can you work with others to double the good consequences of your actions?

_____

_____

_____

_____

_____

_____

_____

_____

_____

_____

_____

_____

_____

_____

_____

_____

_____

7. Can you think of a specific action in your personal or professional life that you've been afraid to take? What inspires or demotivates you to take that action?

_____

_____

_____

_____

_____

_____

_____

_____

_____

The Future of Leadership

Key Lessons:

1. Evolving Leadership Approaches: Chapter 8 explores the transition from top-down to more collaborative and inclusive leadership approaches.

2. Inclusiveness: Inclusive leadership prioritizes the inclusion of various views and viewpoints in decision-making.

3. Disparate leadership positions: The future of leadership will feature shared responsibilities and dispersed leadership positions.

4. Adaptability: In changing circumstances, leaders must be versatile and open to change.

5. Communication and Transparency: In today's world, effective communication and transparency are essential.

6. Values-Driven Leadership: The necessity of integrating leadership with values and ethics is emphasized in this chapter.

7. Ongoing Learning: Future leaders place a premium on self-improvement and ongoing learning.

Self-Reflection Questions

1. What do you think about the evolution of leadership paradigms covered in Chapter 8, and how may it affect your present or future leadership roles?

_____

_____

_____

_____

_____

_____

_____

_____

_____

_____

_____

_____

_____

_____

_____

_____

_____

2. Consider how you handle inclusion in your leadership responsibilities. How do you include other points of view in your decision-making processes?

_____

_____

_____

_____

_____

_____

_____

_____

_____

_____

_____

_____

_____

_____

_____

_____

3. Think about the notion of shared leadership. How comfortable are you with delegating responsibilities and taking on leadership roles? What are the advantages and disadvantages?

_____

_____

_____

_____

_____

_____

_____

_____

_____

_____

_____

_____

_____

_____

_____

4. Consider your versatility as a leader. How adaptable is your leadership style to change and new approaches?

_____

_____

_____

_____

_____

_____

_____

_____

_____

_____

_____

_____

_____

_____

_____

_____

_____

5. Assess your communication methods. Are you encouraging open communication and transparency in your teams or organizations?

_____

_____

_____

_____

_____

_____

_____

_____

_____

_____

_____

_____

_____

_____

_____

_____

_____

_____

6. Think about your principles and ethics. How well do they match your leadership style, and how can you deepen that match?

_____

_____

_____

_____

_____

_____

_____

_____

_____

_____

_____

_____

_____

_____

_____

_____

_____

_____

7. As a leader, how aggressively do you pursue continual learning and self-improvement? What tactics can you put in place to strengthen your commitment to growth?

_____

_____

_____

_____

_____

_____

_____

_____

_____

_____

Self-Assessment Questions

Have you changed your mind about leadership after reading this chapter? If so, how so?

_____

_____

_____

_____

_____

_____

_____

_____

_____

_____

_____

_____

_____

_____

_____

_____

_____

Can you think of any examples of leadership skills you've seen demonstrated outside of typical positions of power in your life?

_____

_____

_____

_____

_____

_____

_____

_____

_____

_____

_____

_____

_____

_____

_____

_____

_____

_____

In your personal and professional lives, how can you use the principle that everyone can be a leader?

_____

_____

_____

_____

_____

_____

_____

_____

_____

_____

_____

_____

_____

_____

_____

_____

_____

Do you feel you already possess any of the attributes presented in this chapter? Which ones do you need to improve?

_____

_____

_____

_____

_____

_____

_____

_____

_____

_____

_____

_____

_____

_____

_____

_____

_____

How well-defined is your personal leadership brand at this moment, and how can you improve it?

_____

_____

_____

_____

_____

_____

_____

_____

_____

_____

_____

_____

_____

_____

_____

_____

_____

_____

Which of the talents discussed in this chapter do you need to enhance or develop further?

_____

_____

_____

_____

_____

_____

_____

_____

_____

_____

_____

_____

_____

_____

_____

_____

Have you identified people in your network who can act as mentors or support your leadership development?

_____

_____

_____

_____

_____

_____

_____

_____

_____

_____

_____

_____

_____

_____

_____

_____

_____

What difficulties have you experienced as a leader, and how have you overcome them?

_____

_____

_____

_____

_____

_____

_____

_____

_____

_____

_____

Checklist

Chapter 1: The Hidden Leader

[ ] Read Chapter 1 thoroughly.

[ ] Reflect on your current definition of leadership.

[ ] Consider examples of leadership outside of traditional positions.

[ ] Note down instances where you've been inspired by unconventional leaders.

Chapter 2: The Qualities of a Great Leader

[ ] Read Chapter 2 carefully.

[ ] Identify the key qualities of a great leader.

[ ] Assess your strengths and areas for improvement regarding these qualities.

[ ] Explore how you can develop and exhibit these qualities in your life.

Chapter 3: Discovering Your Leadership Potential

[ ] Read Chapter 3 and complete the exercises.

[ ] Identify your strengths, weaknesses, and interests.

[ ] Define your personal leadership brand.

[ ] Reflect on your core values and how they relate to your leadership journey.

Chapter 4: Developing Your Leadership Skills

[ ] Read Chapter 4 and engage with the skill development activities.

[ ] Evaluate your current leadership skills.

[ ] Choose specific skills to improve and develop an action plan.

[ ] Explore resources for further skill enhancement.

Chapter 5: Building Your Leadership Network

[ ] Read Chapter 5 and learn about the importance of networking.

[ ] Assess the strength and diversity of your leadership network.

[ ] Identify potential mentors and advisors.

[ ] Plan ways to nurture and expand your network.

Chapter 6: Taking Action and Leading Others

[ ] Read Chapter 6 and absorb insights on taking action as a leader.

[ ] Reflect on your ability to motivate and inspire others.

[ ] Consider how you approach decision-making and empowerment.

[ ] Evaluate your feedback and recognition practices.

Chapter 7: The Power of One

[ ] Read Chapter 7 and explore the concept of individual impact.

[ ] Reflect on instances in your life where small actions created positive change.

[ ] Consider your passions and how they can drive you to make a difference.

[ ] Think about doubts or obstacles you've faced and strategies for overcoming them.

Chapter 8: The Future of Leadership

[ ] Read Chapter 8 and learn about evolving leadership models.

[ ] Reflect on your leadership style in the context of inclusivity and shared leadership.

[ ] Assess your adaptability and communication practices.

[ ] Align your leadership approach with your values and ethics.

[ ] Plan for continuous learning and self-improvement as a leader.

Overall Workbook Completion

[ ] Review your self-reflection responses and any notes you've taken.

[ ] Consider how the key lessons and self-reflection questions have influenced your perspective and actions.

[ ] Think about specific steps you plan to take to become a more effective and inclusive leader.

[ ] Consider sharing your insights and experiences with others who may benefit from the workbook.

This checklist is a useful tool to keep track of your progress and engagement with the book's content, helping you make the most of your journey to becoming a hidden leader.

Conclusion

Finally, this unauthorized workbook is intended to supplement and strengthen your path toward discovering your hidden leader, as detailed in "Unlock The Hidden Leader: Become The Leader You Were Destined To Be." We have covered essential topics, done self-reflection exercises, and offered practical tasks throughout this workbook to help you enhance your leadership abilities, self-awareness, and confidence.

Becoming a leader entail more than just gaining a title or a position; it entails accepting your unique potential and continually working for personal and professional development. You've taken big steps toward fulfilling your leadership potential by working through the activities and reflections in this workbook.

Keep in mind that leadership is a continual process. You will have obstacles and failures along the path, but each one will provide a chance for progress. Continue to practice these activities, seek information, and implement what you've learnt in your daily life. The road to become the leader you were born to be is not always simple, but it is undeniably worthwhile.

We hope that this workbook has been a useful supplement to the book and that it has enabled you to take charge of your leadership path. Your latent leader is ready to emerge, and you may accomplish the leadership greatness you were intended for with determination, self-awareness, and continual learning.

We thank you for starting on this transforming path and wish you every success and fulfillment in your leadership aspirations.

Made in the USA
Las Vegas, NV
22 November 2024

12399614R00056